Why Did You Choose Me? is a perfectly simple way to make any adopted child feel like they are exactly where they need to be! When our daughter asks why we chose her to be a part of our family, even though she looks different than us, this book will be invaluable to communicate our love for her. I am always thankful for books that help to aide us in communicating with our child about adoption.

—SHANNON PATTERSON
Adoptive mom and President of Bethany Christian Services Board in Greenville, SC

As any adoptive parent will tell you, our adopted children do ask many times, "Why did you choose me?" Now my clients who adopt have a fun and colorful resource to touch on and answer this all-important question. Katie Cruice Smith and Sarah Strickling Jones have prepared a learning tool adaptable to a child's early years, which allows an adopted child and her parents to connect on different levels with the topic of adoption. Your child will laugh and smile while learning about adoption, love, and acceptance. I will be buying *Why Did You Choose Me?* for all my adoptive couples!

—RAYMOND W. GODWIN
Father of two adopted daughters and adoption lawyer in Greenville, SC
Co-author of *The Complete Adoption Book*

Why Did You Choose Me? explores a familiar adoption theme, but is pleasantly unpredictable. The illustrations are sure to put a smile on your child's face and your own. Though the book is written in rhyme, the verse is not sing-songy, and the book has just enough sophistication to be enjoyed by everyone.

—DR. DANIEL NEHRBASS
President of Nightlight Christian Adoptions

Why Did You Choose Me? is tender, genuine, and refreshing, and it does this adoptive mom's heart and soul some good. Our daughter, from India, is now asking this very same question proposed in the book. This thoughtfully written and charmingly illustrated book is a great reminder to her of how special and unique she is, and it is a great reminder to her mom (me) of the beautiful gift of adoption. Any family, adopting or not, will be blessed by this sweet story.

—KELLY MCCORKLE PARKISON
Adoptive mom and co-founder of LOFT 218,
Author of *He Knows Her Name*

Why me? is a question we all have asked at one time or another. In *Why Did You Choose Me?*, Katie delightfully and whimsically answers the questions an adoptive child often holds in their heart. When a child goes from a "me" to a "we," an explosion of emotions may happen. Be prepared to share this book and lots of giggles and tears as the words on the pages jumpstart questions of all kinds! Well said, Katie!

—LENNA FOX SMITH, CEO
Piedmont Women's Center in Greenville, SC

Why Did You Choose ME?

Katie Cruice Smith
Illustrated by Sarah Strickling Jones

AMBASSADOR INTERNATIONAL
GREENVILLE, SOUTH CAROLINA & BELFAST, NORTHERN IRELAND

www.ambassador-international.com

Why Did You Choose Me?

Illustrated by Sarah Strickling Jones

ISBN: 978-1-62020-603-4
eISBN: 978-1-62020-676-8

Page Layout: Hannah Nichols
Ebook Conversion: Anna Riebe Raats

AMBASSADOR INTERNATIONAL
Emerald House
411 University Ridge, Suite B14
Greenville, SC 29601, USA
www.ambassador-international.com

AMBASSADOR BOOKS
The Mount
2 Woodstock Link
Belfast, BT6 8DD, Northern Ireland, UK
www.ambassadormedia.co.uk

The colophon is a trademark of Ambassador

Dedicated to the three who call me Mom—
Hannah, Ephraim, and Harmony.
It was no choice for me.
—Katie Cruice Smith

To Darren . . . some day.
—Sarah Strickling Jones

Dear Reader,

During our third adoption, I was applying for every grant that I could find in order to raise money to bring our daughter home. One grant I applied for required that I write an essay answering the question, "If your child came to you one day and asked why you chose them, what would you say?" Fortunately, I won the grant, and the idea began to take root in my mind that this was a question that many children are probably asking.

The truth is that no matter how loving and secure their home may be, many adopted children often question their identity within their family. This book is a way to lovingly and gently answer those questions by showing them that there is no doubt that they were meant to be a part of your family.

Sadly, though, there are still over 130 million children in the world who don't have a loving and secure place to call their own. They don't have a forever family to whom they can ask these questions. To remember each one of these children, we have splashed dots of color throughout the book. My desire is that each one of these children will someday be able to ask these questions of their forever family, too.

Thanks for reading!

Blessings,

Katie

family miracle

hope waiting birth family

forever blessed mother

adoption love

sacrifice child dream

always gift come true

happiness

"Mommy, why did you choose me?"
"My child, don't you know?
From the moment that our hearts met,
I just had to love you so."

"But of all the other children,
You could have chosen one

Who looked a lot more like you
Or was a lot more fun.

Perhaps you could have found someone
Who could juggle bowls upon their head.

Or maybe you could love someone
Who likes to make their bed!

Perhaps you could have chosen
One who always does their chores
And never leaves a great big mess
Hidden behind closet doors!

Perhaps you could have loved someone
Who sings in harmony.

Or maybe you could love someone
Who doesn't climb like a monkey.

Maybe you could have chosen
A more intelligent child
One who is always sweet,
Gentle, good, and mild.

Or maybe you could have chosen one
Who does some magic tricks.

Perhaps you'd like a child who is good at gymnastics.

Maybe you would want a kid who
doesn't pick their nose

Or someone who can't pick up toys or
paper with their toes!

Don't you ever wish, even if just for a day,
That you had chosen someone
Who liked everything your way?"

"Oh, darling, darling child,
You're part of this family!
I didn't care what you looked like,
And you're so much fun to me!

If you could juggle bowls upon your head,

I'd be amazed!

But really anything you do

Is something to be praised.

I'd love for you to make your bed,

But I'm glad the mess belongs to you.

Maybe you can't sing in harmony,

But all I hear is sweet and true.

And though at times, it feels just like
I am living in a zoo,
I really love my animals
Including monkeys, too!

I think that you are super smart,
And I don't want a boring child.
I rather enjoy your spunkiness
And when your imagination runs wild!

I don't need a child who wants to impress
By putting on a show.
And we'll work out your bad habits
As I lovingly help you grow.

Do you think that Mama chose you?
It was no choice for me.
From the moment that I saw you,
I had found my sweet baby."

I would like to thank several people who have made my dream of writing a children's book possible.

First of all, thank you to my wonderful illustrator, Sarah Strickling Jones, who saw my idea for a book and encouraged me to take it to the next level by offering to illustrate it for me. Sarah, without you, this book would still just be an idea in my head. You are always such a blessing to me and a wonderful friend!

Thank you to Sam Lowry, publisher of Ambassador International, who saw that we had a story to tell and decided to support us in our pursuit. To my dear friend and Chief Operating Officer of Ambassador International, Anna Riebe Raats, thank you so much for taking on this project and pushing me to finish it. Without your friendship and support, I would never have known what to do with the story. Thank you for working so hard to promote this book and for your critical eye in keeping me on task! You are one of my favorite people!

Thank you also to Hannah Nichols, our fabulous Creative Director, who put up with all of my edits and offered her thoughts on matching the illustrations with the story. We appreciate your diligence in helping us to see this through and for making our story and illustrations flow together.

A special thank you to my parents, Mike and Susan Cruice, who have encouraged me in my writing for all these years and who have cheered me from the sidelines. Your support has always meant so much to me.

And I couldn't possibly miss thanking my wonderful husband, Jamie, who always stands beside me, telling me that he believes I can do anything I set my mind to. I am so glad that we get to take this journey of adoption together. You are my partner, my love, and my best friend.

Most of all, thank you, Lord, for the gift of adoption. By adopting me as a child of Yours, You have shown me what it really feels like to be loved and secure. May this book be a blessing to others and bring glory to Your Name.

—Katie Cruice Smith

Katie Cruice Smith is a freelance writer, journalist, and editor, and she resides in the Upstate of South Carolina with her husband and three adopted children. Katie is an adoption and foster care advocate, and she and her husband are licensed foster parents and the founders of their church's orphan ministry. She is currently working on a devotional book to accompany *Why Did You Choose Me?*

Sarah Strickling Jones enjoys working with oils, acrylics, ceramics, and printmaking. She creates her artwork and teaches students of all ages from her country home. She lives in Greer, South Carolina, with her husband Darren and four children: Trevor, Peyton, Blake, and Renea. *Why Did You Choose Me?* is Sarah Strickling Jones' first illustrated children's book in watercolor.
You can see more of her work at
www.facebook.com/strickling.jones.studio.

For more information about
Why Did You Choose Me?
please visit:
www.themommyfactor.wordpress.com
authorkatie@charter.net
@authorktcsmith
www.facebook.com/katiecruicesmith

For more information about
AMBASSADOR INTERNATIONAL
please visit:
www.ambassador-international.com
@AmbassadorIntl
www.facebook.com/AmbassadorIntl